MENTAL HEALTH PROBLEMS

ARVIND UPADHYAY

Everyday wellbeing is about how we feel, think and behave. Nobody feels blissfully happy, thinks positive thoughts and behaves sensibly all the time. However, if you are in a pretty good state of mind, it is generally much easier to enjoy life and cope with its challenges.

Looking after your state of mind is just as important as taking care of your body, yet most of us manage our physical health far better than our mental health. As soon as we feel a physical ache or pain we generally try to do something about it, but when we find ourselves feeling very low or stressed we tend to think it is just part and parcel of life and don't do anything to improve the situation.

If you do feel down, anxious or distressed, you are not alone. One in four of us experience a mental health problem in any one year.

The phrase "mental health problems" covers many different conditions, ranging from mild or temporary distress to problems which severely limit a person's ability to cope with everyday life. The move from a mild state of anxiety or depression to a severe one can be very gradual, but it is important to recognise the signs so that action can be taken before the condition becomes serious or prolonged.

Helpful Tips If you do feel down, anxious or distressed, you are not alone. One in four of us experience a mental health problem in any one year.

Contents

I

The Secret of Emotional Wellbeing

10 basic skills for gaining and maintaining emotional wellbeing

1. Set yourself achievable goals Set yourself some goals. Make sure that your goals are specific and achievable. If they are too vague you will never know if you achieved them. If you set them too high you will end up frustrated. Too low, and there will be nothing to aim for. Write down short-term, middle and long-term goals. An example of a short-term goal will concern things to do that day. A middle-term goal could be to make a change to your lifestyle... like deciding to start jogging. A long-term goal might be to learn a new skill, change your job, college etc.

2. Be good to yourself Take notice of your achievements, however small and reward yourself. Think about what gives you pleasure and enjoy the reward. Tell others about your

achievements. Giving time to activities we find rewarding increases our sense of wellbeing, whereas a routine made up almost entirely of things
that we have to do can have the opposite
effect. Doing things to put you in a good
mood is sensible, not self-indulgent; so
don't feel guilty about it.

3. Believe in yourself
Self-confidence is concerned with how we
feel about our abilities. Self-esteem is
slightly different as it reflects the degree to
which we value ourselves. You can build
up your self-confidence and self- esteem
even if it has been low since childhood.

4. Manage your time
Good time management means setting
goals and planning to tackle the most
important things first. Do not waste time on
low priority jobs or spend valuable time on
things outside of your control. Take 5-10
minutes each morning to plan the day.

To build selfconfidence and selfesteem: · Behave as if you're more confident than you feel · Learn from your mistakes · Speak encouragingly to yourself · Do the best you can, but don't try to be perfect · Spend time with people who make you feel good.

Prioritise jobs in this way: A = Absolutely essential B = Better done today C = Could wait D = Delegate/ask someone else to do it 5. Face and solve your problems We all have a tendency to avoid facing our problems. Avoidance is not helpful in the long run because it can make the problem worse, it can create new problems and it stops you getting on with your life and leads to more stress and tension. 6. Keeping things in perspective There is always more than one way of seeing things. This means that although you may not be able to choose the facts, you may be able to choose how you react to them. You can help yourself feel better and be more effective by looking at your situation with an open mind and being realistic about what you can manage.

7. Learning to relax Practising relaxation will give you more energy, decrease anxiety and irritability and reduce pains due to tense muscles. Relaxation time should be seen as an important part of your daily routine.

8. Expressing your feelings Expressing our feelings promotes a sense of wellbeing and freedom from tension. It helps us to recover from hurtful experiences, and also helps other people to understand what is going on inside us. Of course there are times when displays of emotion are not helpful, but hiding or holding back our feelings can cause tensions that affect our physical and mental health.

9. Managing your diet The foods you eat can play an important part in the way you feel, physically and mentally. Too much sugar, coffee or salt can cause tension and irritability, and alcohol is a depressant. For general wellbeing the secret is a balanced diet.

10. Take Exercise Regular exercise is good for us in many ways. It can increase our confidence and self-esteem, stimulate "feel good" chemicals in our bodies, provide an outlet for tension and frustration, relieve anxiety, help us sleep better and prevent some physical illnesses. Choose a sport or exercise you enjoy. Try and go outside each day and enjoy the natural things around you. If you have concerns about your health or fitness speak to your GP. Promoting health in your community Community Lifestyle Officers can help you and your community make positive health and lifestyle changes such as being more active, managing your weight or promoting wellbeing. They are there to work with communities to build on what already

exists locally and create new opportunities for people to improve their health and wellbeing. Problem solving – one step at a time Choose a problem that is causing you concern, then: Write down the problem. Be specific Write down a list of possible solutions Write down the advantages and disadvantages of each solution Choose a solution and break it down into steps Tackle each step, one at a time. If you have more than one problem, write them all down and put them in order of difficulty. Tackle the least difficult problem first.

Helpful Tips Just as achieving physical fitness takes time, practice and commitment, so too does achieving mental fitness.

II
Ways to Well being

Staying healthy is as much about your mind as it is about your body. Here are five very simple things you can do to boost your mood and feel happier.

1. Connect... If you feel isolated and lonely then your mental wellbeing can suffer. Connect with the people around you. Think of these connections as the cornerstones of your life and invest time in developing them. Building these connections will support and enrich you every day.

2. Be active... Getting active is great for your mental wellbeing, as well as your physical health and can improve confidence, reduce stress levels and boost your mood. Go for a walk or run. Step outside. Cycle. Play a game. Garden. Dance

3. Take notice...
Be curious. Be aware of the world around
you and your own thoughts and feelings.
It is perfectly normal in life to experience
stress and anxiety but noticing these
feelings and taking some action can
really help.

4. Keep learning...
Learning new things throughout your
lifetime is good for your brain. It's fun and
can build confidence and self-esteem.

5. Give...
Do something nice for a friend, or a
stranger. Look out, as well as in. Seeing
yourself, and your happiness, linked to the
wider community, can be incredibly
rewarding and creates connections with
the people around you.

Most of us have felt low from time to time, but usually the low mood passes after a few days. Sometimes, a person sinks into depression to a point where they may need professional help to get back to normal. Depression does not mean that you are weak or lazy. It is a common illness like high blood pressure, diabetes or arthritis. It can occur at any age. The good news is that there are things you can do to help yourself and treatments that work well. Signs of depression When we become depressed, we may experience: Loss of identify and self-esteem Sadness, when there is maybe nothing to feel sad about Extreme guilt over minor matters A sense of failure, when this is not realistic

Most of us have felt low from time to time, but usually the low mood passes after a few days. Sometimes, a person sinks into depression to a point where they may need professional help to get back to normal. Depression does not mean that you are weak or lazy. It is a common illness like high blood pressure, diabetes or arthritis. It can occur at any age. The good news is that there are things you can do to help yourself and treatments that work well. Signs of depression When we become depressed, we may experience: Loss of identify and self-esteem Sadness, when there is maybe nothing to feel sad about Extreme guilt over minor matters A sense of failure, when this is not realistic

Coping with depression

Avoid sitting or lying about doing nothing Identify things you used to do regularly and things which you used to enjoy Plan to gradually increase the routine of pleasant activities If a task seems too difficult, try breaking it into a series of small steps Above all reward yourself for your efforts Avoid discussions of bad feelings. Solving problems is more helpful If your appetite is poor, eat small quantities regularly and drink lots of fluids Keep to a normal sleep routine. Avoid daytime naps. At night get up if you are awake for 30 mins or more, and do something that will help you to relax

Managing Depression

If you go off sex, keep some physical closeness with your partner and reassure them it is not personal but a temporary symptom.

Depressive thinking

When you are depressed there are changes in the way you think, as well as in how you feel. You tend to look on the negative side of everything, see the worst in yourself, in your life and your future. Once you are feeling down, you are more likely to remember the bad things that have happened and ignore the good ones. Negative thinking can also trigger depression and it slows down recovery.

Identifying negative thinking

Negative thoughts can be difficult to spot because they become a habit, they can flash quickly into your mind and most of us are not used to noticing our thoughts. Learning to spot and catch these negative thoughts is a skill you can master with time.

Managing Depression

Some examples of negative thinking are: Thinking the worst, eg your boy/girl friend doesn't phone. You assume they don't like you any more Ignoring the positive and only seeing the negative, eg 'The shelves I put up are no good because one screw fell out' Taking things personally and blaming yourself for what others do, eg 'My son failed that exam. I should have helped him more. I am a bad parent'. You may also have beliefs that are unrealistic: I should be happy all the time If someone is hurt by something I say or do, I am a bad person If I show emotion, I am weak If I don't succeed, I am worthless

Changing negative thinking

You can learn to think more positively with You can learn to think more positively with the 3 Step Approach and this will make a huge difference in your life. First, write down your negative thoughts as soon as possible. If it's difficult to notice any thoughts, try noticing when you feel down, and ask 'What went through my mind just before I started feeling sad'. Second, ask yourself 'Is what I believe TRUE?' Ask yourself if everyone would have the same belief Think of other possible explanations for the event Try a different approach. For example, if your friend doesn't phone, call him or her to ask why. Third, balance each unreasonable thought with a more realistic one. These should be different to the unreasonable belief Try to think of realistic statements Try to think of as many alternatives as possible.

Mood Chart

If you are worried about feelings getting out of control, keep track of your feelings, thoughts and behaviour on a "mood chart". This will help you notice anxious or negative thought patterns as soon as they begin, so you can start using your self-help strategies. Make a list of specific feelings, thoughts and behaviour that sometimes apply to you. Only you will know what to put in these lists, but here are some examples: Feelings I am aware of: · Sad · Lonely Thoughts that bother me: · Nobody likes me · I can't cope Negative behaviour: · I'm trying to do too much at once · I'm avoiding people Positive checklist: · I am coping with life · I am in control of my thoughts and feelings Give each of your feelings, thoughts and behaviour a "rating" from 0 to 5. 0 = have not noticed any problems; 5 = things could hardly be any worse. For an example of a mood chart see opposite.

Drugs and Alcohol

Check your drugs and alcohol intake
People who are anxious or depressed may
try to cope with their symptoms by drinking
more alcohol, or using other substances
like cannabis. This makes things worse.
Alcohol
Men and women should not drink more
than 14 units a week on a regular basis*
**Regularly means every day or most days*
of the week.
As a rough guide, there's ONE unit of alcohol in:
half a pint of ordinary strength beer,
lager or cider

one small glass of wine
a single pub measure of spirits.
Spread your drinking over 3 or more days
if you regularly drink as much as 14 units
a week but try to have several alcohol free
days each week.

Managing Stress and Anxiety

It is normal to feel anxious if you are facing something dangerous or difficult, but it is not usual to feel anxious all the time or to feel that anxiety is ruling your life. Severe anxiety is like a "false alarm" – the body over-reacting to something that is not really dangerous. The most noticeable physical signs are nausea, light-headedness, sweating, a racing heart, palpitations and rapid breathing. People often react to severe anxiety by avoiding the situation that makes them feel bad. However, this is not helpful in the long run, because the more you avoid something, the more difficult it will seem to you. It also limits what you can do and does not give you the chance to discover that the situation was not really dangerous after all. Try making a plan to help you face your feared situation, with the least frightening event to be tackled first. When people are under stress, there is also a tendency to worry more than usual. Worry and unrealistic or negative thinking can be triggers for anxiety. People who get anxious sometimes think in ways that bring on the anxiety or make it worse. You may also have beliefs about yourself and about other people that are unrealistic. Anxious people often imagine that other people are judging them harshly. Coping with anxiety Learn to relax and do relaxing things Reduce caffeine and avoid using alcohol Regular physical exercise will help Make a plan to solve problems and take action Change the way you think. Remember you can learn to think more realistically and this will make a huge difference in your life. Use the 3 Step Approach (see Managing Depression). Worry and negative thinking are habits which take time to change .

Anxiety can make you feel breathless. The natural response to this is to breathe in more or to "over breathe". However, this makes the problem worse. The best solution is to slow down your breathing which will stop the unpleasant feelings of anxiety. Remember to breathe in, using your abdomen (not your chest). This is sometimes called stomach breathing, because the abdomen should gently rise and fall rather than your upper chest. Breathe in slowly through your nose to the count of 3 seconds Then slowly breathe out to the count of 3 seconds Pause for 3 seconds before breathing in again Continue this exercise for 5 minutes or so Practise twice a day for 10 minutes (5 minutes is better than nothing)

Try to check and slow down your breathing during the day Use the slow breathing technique whenever you get anxious. Relaxation Exercise Before starting this exercise it is advised to talk to your GP about the pros and cons of gently tensing muscles. This particularly applies to people with high blood pressure or a history of heart problems. Choose a quiet place where you will not be interrupted Before you start, do a few gentle stretching exercises to relieve muscular tension Make yourself comfortable, whether sitting or lying down Start to breathe slowly and deeply, in a calm, effortless way

Gently tense, then relax, each part of your body, starting with your feet and working your way up to your face and head As you focus on each area, think of warmth, heaviness and relaxation Push any distracting thoughts to the back of your mind; imagine them floating away Don't try to relax; simply let go of the tension in your muscles and allow them to become relaxed Let your mind go empty. Some people find it helpful to visualise a calm, beautiful place like a garden or meadow. Stay like this for about 20 minutes. Then take some deep breaths and open your eyes, but stay sitting or lying for a few moments before you get up.

Panic attacks are very frightening because they seem to come out of the blue. Most people describe a sudden, overwhelming sense of anxiety, including: Feelings of absolute terror Very rapid breathing and heartbeat Dizziness or faintness Sweating and hot or cold flushes Feelings of unreality. Coping with a panic attack Slow your breathing Stay where you are Remind yourself that you are safe and that the feeling will pass Try to distract yourself by looking hard at something nearby Face the situation again later.

Managing Anger

Anger
Anger needs to be expressed, because if it
gets bottled up inside it can cause harm or

*boil over into rage. You are 6 times more
likely to suffer from heart disease if you
are persistently angry. Anger has to be
expressed calmly, not aggressively.
Remember that losing your temper is never
a good solution. It may provide temporary
relief, but later on you will feel bad, which
can lead to more anger.
First aid for anger
Breathe slowly and deeply
Slow down. Don't rush into words or
actions you may regret
Count to 10
Walk away if possible
Do something physical like a vigorous
walk or housework
Take some exercise but not a
competitive sport as this can
increase feelings of aggression.*

*How to tackle deeper, long-term feelings of anger Talk to
someone about the way you feel Ask your GP for help in
tackling your feelings If it is yourself you are angry with,
think whether you are blaming yourself unfairly Try to think
about the bigger picture Express your feelings in writing or
painting Practice techniques to make yourself more relaxed
and stress-free Don't take things personally Recognise your
own early warning signs.
If you want to deal with your anger STOP blaming others
and START to change yourself*

Self Help

When concerned about your emotional health there is a lot you can do to help yourself. Help can also be found from families, friends and work colleagues. An important thing to accept is that there are usually no instant solutions to problems in life. Solving problems involves time, energy and work. When you are feeling depressed, you may not be feeling energetic or motivated to work. But if you are able to take an active part in your treatment, it should help your situation. Self-help creates self-determination. There may come a time when you feel you might benefit from additional help. Details of professional help can be found in this booklet, together with a list of local and national organisations that are there to help you. For more self help options see the 'Suggested Reading' on page 38 and the list of useful organisations, apps and websites at the back of this booklet. Here are some steps you may want to take in managing your problems: Support from your GP Surgery There are many sources of help to be found via your surgery. A GP is many people's first point of contact when seeking help - a sizeable proportion of most GPs work is related to emotional problems. GPs can: Talk through your problems with you Talk about other sources of help in the community Prescribe medication Refer you to the Somerset Partnership Talking Therapies Refer you to specialist mental health services .

Your Practice Nurse, Health Visitor or District Nurse may also be able to help you manage your mental health difficulties and discuss options available in your surgery and community. Medication Sometimes when a person's distress is acute, their GP may prescribe medication. Some people dislike the idea of taking medication, believing they should be able to manage without, but there are times when it is the best solution. Taking medication on its own is beneficial and it can help you benefit from other treatments. All medication has some side effects – usually minor but it is very important to not stop taking medication without consulting your doctor.

Professional Help

Somerset Partnership Talking Therapies Service Many people, at some time in their life, will experience difficult emotional problems or psychological distress such as anxiety, stress or depression. This is a free and confidential psychological therapies service for people who are 18 years and over. They offer a variety of treatment approaches to meet a range of people's emotional needs. Staff are trained in effective psychological interventions to help you move towards recovery. These include self-help, guided self help, psycho-educational courses and problemfocussed courses. If problems remain, some 1-1 therapy is available, such as Cognitive Behavioural Therapy (CBT) and Counselling.

What kind of difficulties can the service help you with? Anxiety or worry about your health Depression and low self-esteem Excessive worrying Extreme shyness and social phobia Loss and Adjustment Obsessive Compulsive disorder Panic and agoraphobia Problems after a traumatic event Specific phobias Stress and work related problems Body Image and eating difficulties

Types of interventions available:

Telephone assessment and triage
Targeted Self-Help including materials
for depression, stress, anxiety and
childhood sexual abuse
Psycho-educational courses to help
you learn skills to deal with your
difficulties and meet other people
struggling with similar issues.
They have courses to help with: low
mood, stress and anxiety; self-esteem;
assertiveness; loss and adjustment
and managing your anger
Telephone sessions with skilled
workers guiding you through
self help materials based on CBT
Sessions focussing on sleep hygiene,
medication management, low
mood, anxiety, stress
Advice and information including other
organisations that can help
Cognitive Behavioural Therapy
Psychological Therapy

Specialist mental health services Sometimes when problems become severe or people are at risk, your GP will talk to you about referral to your local specialist mental health service. This is a team of mental health staff including a Psychiatrist, Community Psychiatric Nurses (CPN), Clinical Psychologist, Social Worker, and other support staff. They are skilled and experienced in managing complex problems in a professional, confidential and sensitive manner.

If someone close to you is experiencing emotional problems, encourage them to talk about their feelings and, if necessary, get advice from their GP. They may need a lot of support and their behaviour can be out of character and worrying. You can help by listening. Be reassuring and encouraging, but try not to tell them how they should feel or what they should do. Show appreciation, small successes should be recognised and celebrated. Anything that may help the person forget their problems for a while is beneficial. Practical help may be needed short term with everyday tasks. It can be very upsetting when a friend or relative is distressed, and you may well find yourself in a caring role that you did not choose. Ask friends and relatives for help. Outside support may also be helpful. Remember your emotional wellbeing is important too! See the Carers organisations listed at the back of the book.

III

Mental health in Europe

Countries in the WHO European Region face enormous challenges in working to promote the mental well-being of their populations, to prevent mental health problems in marginalized and vulnerable groups and to treat, care for and support the recovery of people with mental health problems. Mental health has growing priority across the Region, owing to the awareness of both the human and economic costs to society and the suffering of individuals. The WHO European Ministerial Conference on Mental Health, held in Helsinki in January 2005, identifi ed the main issues to be tackled, and viable solutions that can be implemented in all countries, regardless of their stage of mental health development. This book presents the two main results of the Conference: the Mental Health Declaration and Action Plan for Europe, which were adopted by the Member States in the Region and enshrine their commitment to improve mental health. Then follow 14 briefi ngs on the areas of work in the Action Plan, including examples of successful interventions, and a brief description of the way forward for the mental health programme of the WHO Regional Offi ce for Europe in assisting Member States to reach the ambitious goals they have set for themselves. This chapter, however, describes the current situation in the Region – and the challenge to which countries are responding through the Declaration and Action

Plan. Burden Mental health is currently one of the biggest challenges facing every country in the Region, with mental health problems affecting at least one in four people at some time in their lives. The prevalence of mental health disorders is very high in Europe. Of the 870 million people living in the European Region, at any one time about 100 million people are estimated to suffer from anxiety and depression; over 21 million to suffer from alcohol use disorders; over 7 million from Alzheimer's disease and other dementias; about 4 million from schizophrenia; 4 million from bipolar affective disorder; and 4 million from panic disorders. Neuropsychiatric disorders are the second greatest cause of the burden of disease on the Region after cardiovascular diseases. They account for 19.5% of all disability-adjusted life-years (DALYs – years lost to ill health and premature death). Depression alone is the third greatest cause, accounting for 6.2% of all DALYs. Self-infl icted injuries are the eleventh leading cause of DALYs, accounting for 2.2%. Alzheimer's disease and other dementias are the fourteenth leading cause of DALYs, accounting for 1.9%. The number of people with these disorders is likely to increase further as the population ages. Neuropsychiatric disorders also account for over 40% of chronic disease and are the greatest cause of years lived with disability. Depression is the single most important cause. Five of the highest fi fteen contributors are mental disorders. In many countries, mental health problems account for 35–45% of absenteeism from work. One of the most tragic results of mental health problems is suicide. Nine of the ten countries in the world with the highest rates of suicide are in the European Region. The most recent available data show that about 150 000 people, of whom 80% are male, commit suicide every year. Suicide is a leading and hidden cause of death among young adults, second only to traffi c accidents among those aged 15–35 years. Stigma and discrimination Too often, the widespread stigma attached to mental health problems jeopardizes the development and implementation of mental health policy. Stigma is the main cause of discrimination and exclusion: it affects people's self-esteem, helps to disrupt their family relationships, and limits their ability to socialize and get housing and jobs. It also contributes to the abuse of human rights in some large institutions. Mental health promotion Governments now recognize the importance of mental well-being for all citizens. It is fundamental to the quality of life, enabling people to experience life as meaningful and to be creative and active. Public mental health reinforces lifestyles conducive to mental well-being. Mental health promotion needs to target the whole population, including people with mental health problems and their carers. The development and implementation of effective plans to promote mental health will enhance mental well-being for all. Prevention of harmful stress and suicide People in many countries are exposed to harmful stress that leads to an increase in anxiety and depression, alcohol and other substance use disorders, violence and suicidal behaviour. Countries are now aware of the potential benefi ts of activities to reduce harmful stress and the importance of reducing suicide rates. The social causes of mental health problems are manifold, ranging from individual causes of distress to issues that affect a whole community or society. They can be induced or reinforced in many different settings, including the home, educational facilities, the workplace and institutions. Marginalized and vulnerable groups – such as refugees and migrant populations, and people who are unemployed, in or leaving prisons, have different sexual orientations, have disabilities or are already experiencing mental health problems – can be at particular risk. Services In many instances, care based in the community has been shown to offer a better quality of life and greater satisfaction for service users and their families than traditional hospital care. Across the Region, bed numbers are falling and institutions are being closed down, but the pace of change is uneven. Institutional care still dominates in most parts of the Region. In a quarter of European countries, mental health services are not available in the community. In some countries, over 50% of all patients are treated in large mental hospitals. Indeed, more than two thirds of all mental hospital beds in Europe are in psychiatric hospitals. In some countries, 85% of the money devoted to mental health is spent on maintaining large institutions. In over one third, treatment for severe mental health disorders is not available from family doctors and there are no mental health training programmes for family doctors or other primary health care professionals. One fi fth of countries do not make the three essential psychotropic drugs (amitriptyline, chlorpromazine and phenytoin) available in primary health care. One fi fth also do not have a therapeutic drug policy or an essential drug list. The quality of care depends heavily on the quality of the workforce. The signifi cant variations between countries in the number of mental health professionals arouses concern: · the number of psychiatrists ranges from 1.8 to 25 per 100 000 population; · the number of psychiatric nurses ranges from 3 to 104 per 100 000 population; · the number of psychologists ranges from 0.1 to 96 per 100 000 population. Treatment gap A vast gap exists between the need for treatment and the services available. In a European Union survey published in 2003, 90% of people who said they had mental health problems reported they had received no care or treatment in the previous 12 months. Only 2.5% of them had seen a psychiatrist or psychologist. Even in developed countries with well-organized health care systems, between 44% and 70% of patients with mental health disorders do not receive treatment. For example, in western Europe alone, evidence indicates that about 45% of people suffering from depression get no treatment. Cost and fi nancing Mental health disorders cost national economies billions of dollars in terms of expenditure and loss of productivity. Human and economic costs also fall on people with mental health disorders and their families, whose lives can be severely affected. All countries in the European Region must work with limited resources, but their mental health budgets constitute on average only 5.8% of their total health expenditure, while ranging from about 0.1% to 12%. A large proportion of these budgets is allocated to services, and only negligible amounts invested in promotion and prevention.

IV
Mental Health Action Plan for Europe

This Action Plan is endorsed in the Mental Health Declaration for Europe by ministers of health of the Member States in the WHO European Region. They support its implementation in accordance with each country's needs and resources. The challenges over the next fi ve to ten years are to develop, implement and evaluate policies and legislation that will deliver mental health activities capable of improving the well-being of the whole population, preventing mental health problems and enhancing the inclusion and functioning of people experiencing mental health problems. The priorities for the next decade are to: i. foster awareness of the importance of mental well-being; ii. collectively tackle stigma, discrimination and inequality, and empower and support people with mental health problems and their families to be actively engaged in this process; iii. design and implement comprehensive, integrated and effi cient mental health systems that cover promotion, prevention, treatment and rehabilitation, care and recovery; iv. address the need for a competent workforce, effective in all these areas; v. recognize the experience and knowledge of service users and carers2 as an important basis for planning and developing services.

This Action Plan proposes ways and means of developing, implementing and reinforcing comprehensive mental health policies in the countries of the WHO European Region, requiring action in the 12 areas as set out below. Countries will refl ect these policies in their own mental health strategies and plans, to determine what will be delivered over the next fi ve and ten years. 1. Promote mental well-being for all Challenge Mental health and well-being are fundamental to quality of life, enabling people to experience life as meaningful and to be creative and active citizens. Mental health is an essential component of social cohesion, productivity and peace and stability in the living environment, contributing to social capital and economic development in societies. Public mental health and lifestyles conducive to mental well-being are crucial to achieving this aim. Mental health promotion increases the quality of life and mental well-being of the whole population, including people with mental health problems and their carers. The development and implementation of effective plans to promote mental health will enhance mental well-being for all. Actions to consider i. Develop comprehensive strategies for mental health promotion within the context of mental health, public health and other public policies that address the promotion of mental health across the lifespan. ii. Adopt promotion of mental health as a long-term investment and develop education and information programmes with a long time frame. iii. Develop and offer effective programmes for parenting support and education, starting during pregnancy. iv. Develop and offer evidence-based programmes that foster skills, provide information and focus on resilience, emotional intelligence and psychosocial functioning in children and young people. v. Improve access to healthy diets and physical activity for older people. vi. Promote community-based multilevel interventions involving public awareness campaigns, primary care staff and community facilitators such as teachers, clergy and the media. vii. Integrate mental health promotion components into existing generic health promotion and public health policies and programmes, such as those supported by WHO health promoting networks. viii. Encourage the consumption of healthy products and reduce the intake of harmful products. ix. Create healthy workplaces by introducing measures such as exercise, changes to work patterns, sensible hours and healthy management styles. x. Offer effective mental health promotion activities to groups at risk such as people with enduring mental or physical health problems and carers. xi. Identify clear mechanisms for empowering the population to take responsibility for health promotion and disease prevention targets, for example by heightening public awareness of the importance of life choices. 2. Demonstrate the centrality of mental health Challenge Mental health is central to building a healthy, inclusive and productive society. Sound and integrated public policies, such as those on labour, urban planning and socioeconomic issues, also have a positive impact on mental health and reduce the risk of mental health problems. The mental health implications of all public policy, and particularly its potential impact on groups at risk, therefore need to be considered. Mental health policy requires intersectoral linkages and should incorporate multisectoral and multidisciplinary approaches. Actions to consider i. Make mental health an inseparable part of public health. ii. Incorporate a mental health perspective and relevant actions into new and existing national policies and legislation. iii. Include mental health in programmes dealing with occupational health and safety. iv. Assess the potential impact of any new policy on the mental well-being of the population before its introduction and evaluate its results afterwards. v. Give special consideration to the relative impact of policies on people already suffering from mental health problems and those at risk. 3. Tackle stigma and discrimination Challenge Mental health policy development and implementation must not be jeopardized by the widespread stigma attached to mental health problems that leads to discrimination. In many instances, people with mental health problems suffer from a lack of equal opportunities because of such discrimination. Human rights and respect for people with mental health problems must be protected. Empowerment is a crucial step towards meeting these objectives, as it enhances integration and social inclusion. The lack of empowerment of service users' and carers' organizations and poor advocacy hinder the design and implementation of policies and activities that are sensitive to their needs and wishes. The exclusion experienced by mental health service users, whether in asylums and institutions or in the community, needs to be tackled in a variety of ways. Actions to consider i. Instigate activities to counter stigma and discrimination, emphasizing the ubiquity of mental health problems, their general good prognosis and treatability, and the fact that they are rarely associated with violence. ii. Introduce or scrutinize disability rights legislation to ensure that it covers mental health equally and equitably. iii. Develop and implement national, sectoral and enterprise policies to eliminate stigma and discrimination in employment practices associated with mental health problems.iv. Stimulate community involvement in local mental health programmes by supporting initiatives of nongovernmental organizations. v. Develop a coherent programme of policy and legislation to address stigma and discrimination, incorporating international and regional human rights standards. vi. Establish constructive dialogue with the media and systematically provide them with information. vii. Set standards for representation of users and their carers on committees and groups responsible for planning, delivery, review and inspection of mental health activities. viii. Stimulate the creation and development of local and national nongovernmental and service-user-run organizations representing people with mental health problems, their carers and the communities they live in. ix. Encourage the integration of children and young people with mental health problems and disabilities in the regular educational and vocational training system. x. Establish vocational training for people suffering from mental health problems and support the adaptation of workplaces and working practices to their special needs, with the aim of securing their entry into competitive employment. 4. Promote activities sensitive to vulnerable life stages Challenge Infants, children and young people, and older people are particularly at risk from social, psychological, biological and environmental factors. Given their vulnerability and needs, young and older people should be a high priority for activities related to the promotion of mental health and the prevention and care of mental health problems. However, many countries have inadequate capacity in this area, and services and staff are often poorly prepared to deal with developmental and age-related problems. In particular, disorders in childhood can be important precursors of adult mental disorders. Supporting the mental health of children and adolescents should be seen as a strategic investment that creates many longterm benefi ts for individuals, societies and health systems. Actions to consider i. Ensure that policies on mental health include as priorities the mental health and well-being of children and adolescents and of older people. ii. Incorporate the international rights of children and adolescents and of older people into mental health legislation. iii. Involve young people and older people as much as possible in the decisionmaking process.

iv. Pay special attention to marginalized groups, including children and older people from migrant families. v. Develop mental health services sensitive to the needs of young and older people, operated in close collaboration with families, schools, day-care centres, neighbours, extended families and friends. vi. Promote the development of community centres for older people to increase social support and access to interventions. vii. Ensure that age- and gender-sensitive mental health services are provided by both primary care and specialized health and social care services and operate as integrated networks. viii. Restrict institutional approaches for the care of children and adolescents and older people that engender social exclusion and neglect. ix. Improve the quality of dedicated mental health services by establishing or improving the capacity for specialized interventions and care in childhood and adolescence and old age, and by training and employing adequate numbers of specialists. x. Improve coordination between organizations involved in alcohol and drugs programmes and children's and adolescents' health and mental health at the national and international levels, as well as collaboration between their respective networks. xi. Ensure parity of funding in relation to comparable health services. 5. Prevent mental health problems and suicide Challenge People in many countries are exposed to harmful stress-inducing societal changes that affect social cohesion, safety and employment and lead to an increase in anxiety and depression, alcohol and other substance use disorders, violence and suicidal behaviour. The social precipitants of mental health problems are manifold and can range from individual causes of distress to issues that affect a whole community or society. They can be induced or reinforced in many different settings, including the home, educational facilities, the workplace and institutions. Marginalized and vulnerable groups, such as refugees and migrant populations, the unemployed, people in or leaving prisons, people with different sexual orientations, people with physical and sensorial disabilities and people already experiencing mental health problems, can be particularly at risk. Actions to consider i. Increase awareness of the prevalence, symptoms and treatability of harmful stress, anxiety, depression and schizophrenia.

ii. Target groups at risk, offering prevention programmes for depression, anxiety, harmful stress, suicide and other risk areas, developed on the basis of their specifi c needs and sensitive to their background and culture. iii. Establish self-help groups, telephone help-lines and web sites to reduce suicide, particularly targeting high-risk groups. iv. Establish policies that reduce the availability of the means to commit suicide. v. Introduce routine assessment of the mental health of new mothers by obstetricians and health visitors and provide interventions where necessary. vi. For families at risk, provide home-based educational interventions to help proactively to improve parenting skills, health behaviour and interaction between parents and children. vii. Set up in partnership with other ministers evidence-based education programmes addressing suicide, depression, alcohol and other substance use disorders for young people at schools and universities and involve role models and young people in the making of campaigns. viii. Support the implementation of community development programmes in high-risk areas and empower nongovernmental agencies, especially those representing marginalized groups. ix. Ensure adequate professional support and services for people encountering major crises and violence, including war, natural disasters and terrorist attacks in order to prevent post-traumatic stress disorder. x. Increase awareness among staff employed in health care and related sectors of their own attitudes and prejudices towards suicide and mental health problems. xi. Monitor work-related mental health through the development of appropriate indicators and instruments. xii. Develop the capacities for protection and promotion of mental health at work through risk assessment and management of stress and psychosocial factors, training of personnel, and awareness raising. xiii. Involve mainstream agencies responsible for employment, housing and education in the development and delivery of prevention programmes. 6. Ensure access to good primary care for mental health problems Challenge For many countries in the European Region, general practitioners (GPs) and other primary care staff are the initial and main source of help for common mental health problems. However, mental health problems often remain undetected in people attending GPs or primary care services and treatment is not always adequate when they are identifi ed. Many people with mental health problems, particularly those who are vulnerable or marginalized, experience diffi culties in accessing and remaining in contact with services. GPs and primary care services need to develop capacity and competence to detect and treat people with mental health problems in the community, supported as required as part of a network with specialist mental health services. Actions to consider i. Ensure that all people have good access to mental health services in primary health care settings. ii. Develop primary care services with the capacity to detect and treat mental health problems, including depression, anxiety, stress-related disorders, substance misuse and psychotic disorders as appropriate by expanding the numbers and skills of primary care staff. iii. Provide access to psychotropic medication and psychotherapeutic interventions in primary care settings for common as well as severe mental disorders, especially for individuals with long-term and stable mental disorders who are resident in the community. iv. Encourage primary health care staff to take up mental health promotion and prevention activities, particularly targeting factors that determine or maintain ill health. v. Design and implement treatment and referral protocols in primary care, establishing good practice and clearly defi ning the respective responsibilities in networks of primary care and specialist mental health services. vi. Create centres of competence and promote networks in each region which health professionals, service users, carers and the media can contact for advice. vii. Provide and mainstream mental health care in other primary care services and in easily accessible settings such as community centres and general hospitals. 7. Offer effective care in community-based services for people with severe mental health problems Challenge Progress is being made across the Region in reforming mental health care. It is essential to acknowledge and support people's right to receive the most effective treatments and interventions while being exposed to the lowest possible risk, based on their individual wishes and needs and taking into account their culture, religion, gender and aspirations. Evidence and experience in many countries support the development of a network of community-based services including hospital beds. There is no place in the twenty-fi rst century for inhumane and degrading treatment and care in large institutions: an increasing number of countries have closed many of their asylums and are now implementing effective communitybased services. Special consideration should be given to the emotional, economic and educational needs of families and friends, who are often responsible for intensive support and care and often require support themselves. Actions to consider i. Empower service users and carers to access mental health and mainstream services and to take responsibility for their care in partnership with providers. ii. Plan and implement specialist community-based services, accessible 24 hours a day, 7 days a week, with multidisciplinary staff, to care for people with severe problems such as schizophrenia, bipolar disorder, severe depression or dementia. iii. Provide crisis care, offering services where people live and work, preventing deterioration or hospital admission whenever possible, and only admitting people with very severe needs or those who are a risk to themselves or others. iv. Offer comprehensive and effective treatments, psychotherapies and medications with as few side effects as possible in community settings, particularly for young people experiencing a fi rst episode of mental health problems. v. Guarantee access to necessary medicines for people with mental health problems at a cost that the health care system and the individual can afford, in order to achieve appropriate prescription and use of these medicines. vi. Develop rehabilitation services that aim to optimize people's inclusion in society, while being sensitive to the impact of disabilities related to mental health problems. vii. Offer services for people with mental health needs who are in nonspecialist settings such as general hospitals or prisons. viii. Offer carers and families assessment of their emotional and economic needs, and involvement in care programmes. ix. Design programmes to develop the caring and coping skills and competencies of families and carers. x. Scrutinize whether benefi t programmes take account of the economic cost of caring. xi. Plan and fund model programmes that can be used for dissemination. xii. Identify and support leaders respected by their peers to spearhead innovation. xiii. Develop guidelines for good practice and monitor their implementation.

xiv. Introduce legal rights for people subject to involuntary care to choose their independent advocate. xv. Introduce or reinforce legislation or regulations protecting the standards of care, including the discontinuation of inhuman and degrading care and interventions. xvi. Establish inspection to reinforce good practice and to stop neglect and abuse in mental health care. 8. Establish partnerships across sectors Challenge Essential services, which in the past were routinely provided in large institutions or were not considered as relevant to the lives of people with mental health problems, are nowadays often fragmented across many agencies. Poor partnership and lack of coordination between services run or funded by different agencies lead to poor care, suffering and ineffi ciencies. The responsibilities of different bodies for such a wide range of services need coordination and leadership up to and including government level. Service users and their carers need support in accessing and receiving services for issues such as benefi ts, housing, meals, employment and treatment for physical conditions, including substance misuse. Actions to consider i. Organize comprehensive preventive and care services around the needs of and in close cooperation with users. ii. Create collaborative networks across services that are essential to the quality of life of users and carers, such as social welfare, labour, education, justice, transport and health. iii. Give staff in mental health services responsibility for identifying and providing support for needs in daily living activities, either by direct action or through coordination with other services. iv. Educate staff in other related services about the specifi c needs and rights of people with mental health problems and those at risk of developing mental health problems. v. Identify and adjust fi nancial and bureaucratic disincentives that obstruct collaboration, including at government level. 9. Create a suffi cient and competent workforce Challenge Mental health reform demands new staff roles and responsibilities, requiring changes in values and attitudes, knowledge and skills. The working practices of many mental health care workers and staff in other sectors such as teachers,benefi t offi cers, the clergy and volunteers need to be modernized in order to offer effective and effi cient care. New training opportunities must respond to the need for expertise in all roles and tasks to be undertaken. Actions to consider i. Recognize the need for new staff roles and responsibilities across the specialist and generic workforce employed in the health service and other relevant areas such as social welfare and education. ii. Include experience in community settings and multidisciplinary teamwork in the training of all mental health staff. iii. Develop training in the recognition, prevention and treatment of mental health problems for all staff working in primary care. iv. Plan and fund, in partnership with educational institutions, programmes that address the education and training needs of both existing and newly recruited staff. v. Encourage the recruitment of new mental health workers and enhance the retention of existing workers. vi. Ensure an equitable distribution of mental health workers across the population, particularly among people at risk, by developing incentives. vii. Address the issue of lack of expertise in new technologies of present trainers, and support the planning of "train the trainers" programmes. viii. Educate and train mental health staff about the interface between promotion, prevention and treatment. ix. Educate the workforce across the public sector to recognize the impact of their policies and actions on the mental health of the population. x. Create an expert workforce by designing and implementing adequate specialist mental health training for all staff working in mental health care. xi. Develop specialist training streams for areas requiring high levels of expertise such as the care and treatment of children, older people and people suffering from a combination of mental health problems and substance use disorder (comorbidity).

Actions to consider i. Develop or strengthen a national surveillance system based on internationally standardized, harmonized and comparable indicators and data collection systems, to monitor progress towards local, national and international objectives of improved mental health and well-being. ii. Develop new indicators and data collection methods for information not yet available, including indicators of mental health promotion, prevention, treatment and recovery. iii. Support the carrying out of periodic population-based mental health surveys, using agreed methodology across the WHO European Region. iv. Measure base rates of incidence and prevalence of key conditions, including risk factors, in the population and groups at risk. v. Monitor existing mental health programmes, services and systems. vi. Support the development of an integrated system of databases across the WHO European Region to include information on the status of mental health policies, strategies, implementation and delivery of evidence-based promotion, prevention, treatment, care and recovery. vii. Support the dissemination of information on the impact of good policy and practice nationally and internationally. 11. Provide fair and adequate funding Challenge Resources dedicated to mental health are often inadequate and inequitable compared to those available to other parts of the public sector, and this is refl ected in poor access, neglect and discrimination. In some health care systems, insurance coverage of access and rights to treatment discriminate severely against mental health problems. Within the mental health budget, resource allocation should be equitable and proportionate, i.e. offering greatest relative share and benefi ts to those in greatest need. Actions to consider i. Assess whether the proportion of the health budget allocated to mental health fairly refl ects the needs and priority status of the people with needs. ii. Ensure that people with the most severe problems and the poorest in society receive the largest relative benefi ts. iii. Assess whether funding is allocated effi ciently, taking into account societal benefi ts, including those generated by promotion, prevention and care.

iv. Evaluate whether coverage is comprehensive and fair in social and private insurance-based systems, on an equal level to that for other conditions, not excluding or discriminating against groups and particularly protecting the most vulnerable. 12. Evaluate effectiveness and generate new evidence Challenge Considerable progress is being made in research, but some strategies and interventions still lack the necessary evidence base, meaning that further investment is required. Furthermore, investment in dissemination is also required, since the existing evidence concerning effective new interventions and national and international examples of good practice are not known to many policy-makers, managers, practitioners and researchers. The European research community needs to collaborate to lay the foundations for evidence-based mental health activities. Major research priorities include mental health policy analyses, assessments of the impact of generic policies on mental health, evaluations of mental health promotion programmes, a stronger evidence base for prevention activities and new service models and mental health economics. Actions to consider i. Support national research strategies that identify, develop and implement best practice to address the needs of the population, including groups at risk. ii. Evaluate the impact of mental health systems over time and apply experiences to the formulation of new priorities and the commissioning of the necessary research. iii. Support research that facilitates the development of preventive programmes aimed at the whole population, including groups at risk. Research is needed on the implications of the interrelated nature of many mental, physical and social health problems for effective preventive programmes and policies. iv. Promote research focused on estimating the health impacts of non-health sector policies, as there is a clear potential for positive mental health to be improved through such policies. v. Bridge the knowledge gap between research and practice by facilitating collaboration and partnerships between researchers, policy-makers and practitioners in seminars and accessible publications. vi. Ensure that research programmes include long-term evaluations of impact not only on mental health but also on physical health, as well as social and economic effects.

vii. Establish sustainable partnerships between practitioners and researchers for the implementation and evaluation of new or existing interventions. viii. Invest in training in mental health research across academic disciplines, including anthropology, sociology, psychology, management studies and economics, and create incentives for long-term academic partnerships. ix. Expand European collaboration in mental health research by enhancing networking between WHO's European collaborating centres and other centres with research activities in the fi eld of prevention. x. Invest in regional collaboration on information and dissemination in order to avoid the duplication of generally applicable research and ignorance of successful and relevant activities elsewhere. Mental health for Europe: facing the challenges Milestones Member States are committed, through the Mental Health Declaration for Europe and this Action Plan, to face the challenges by moving towards the following milestones. Between 2005 and 2010 they should: 1. prepare policies and implement activities to counter stigma and discrimination and promote mental well-being, including in healthy schools and workplaces; 2. scrutinize the mental health impact of public policy; 3. include the prevention of mental health problems and suicide in national policies; 4. develop specialist services capable of addressing the specifi c challenges of the young and older people, and gender-specifi c issues; 5. prioritize services that target the mental health problems of marginalized and vulnerable groups, including problems of comorbidity, i.e. where mental health problems occur jointly with other problems such as substance misuse or physical illness; 6. develop partnership for intersectoral work and address disincentives that hinder joint work; 7. introduce human resource strategies to build up a suffi cient and competent mental health workforce; 8. defi ne a set of indicators on the determinants and epidemiology of mental health and for the design and delivery of services in partnership with other Member States; 9. confi rm health funding, regulation and legislation that is equitable and inclusive of mental health; 10. end inhumane and degrading treatment and care and enact human rights and mental health legislation to comply with the standards of United Nations conventions and international legislation; 11. increase the level of social inclusion of people with mental health problems; 12. ensure representation of users and carers on committees and groups responsible for the planning, delivery, review and inspection of mental health activities.

• 41 •